AF322595

MONSTERS THAT BRUSH MY HAIR

Monsters That Brush My Hair

A collection of poems

DAWN SOLIS

CONTENTS

COPYRIGHT

DEDICATION

To my family
We are stronger together

~ 1 ~

MONSTERS

Monsters don't sleep under the bed.
They sleep inside your head.
Monsters don't tell you that you're a terrible person, they just
ask you questions about yourself until you question your own
reality.
Monsters are not *bad*.
They just change the panels of light until you cannot remember
the last time you saw the sun.
Monsters are not a figment of our imagination but it is us. *Our-
selves.*
Monsters provide you with so much truth it overwhelms.

~ 2 ~

PAY ATTENTION TO ME

Pay attention to me, please.
Look at me!
Find the scars that I desperately try to keep hidden.
Look and *see* the tears that I hastily wipe away.
Find the notes that I have written.
Find the band-aids I have used.
Look and *see* the loneliness and desperation on my face.
Look and see.
Look and *find*.
Maybe then you can force me to stay.
You can force me to live.
You can force me to leave the knife.
The pills,
the rope.
Pay attention to me please.
I can't do this by myself.
I can't live of my own free will.
So pay attention,
And force me to stay.

~ 3 ~

MY DEMEANOR

I'm a naturally angry person.
Anger has always been a primary emotion for me.
For years, I've pushed it down, and away.
It cracked my bones from the inside out.
I am starting to realize that maybe being angry isn't a bad
thing.
They say that tears are cleansing, "*Let it all out*".
But when it's out what is left?
Instead of being hurt, and upset, *anger* fuels my blood.
Instead of thinking, "What did I do wrong?",
I think, "You can leave. They all do. It's not like this hasn't
happened before".
Now, instead of tears washing out my train of thought I realize
they all say the same sweet sentiments, but *never* have they
followed through.
I'm too mean, and I'm *okay with that*.
I refuse to apologize for how I choose to repair what you broke.
Too rough around the edges, and that stops me from being
ripped apart myself.
No more am I going to allow myself to be pained by other
people's losses.

They never talk about how emotionally aggravating it is to see
the same patterned repeated over and *over*.
There are times where you just have to be *mean*.
No one survives in this world with a kind heart, not really.
Persephone was the goddess of spring, and flowers
Until her mother broke her heart and she sent the world into
winter.
I am not broken because I am angry.
I am broken because you broke me, and I repaired myself with
rusted nails and a titanium fence.
I am *whole*, in my anger.

~ 4 ~

GLASS CEILING

You're tired.
This year has been hard.
Exhausting.
Awful.
You've tried so much and pushed so hard that the glass broke in
your hand.
As you try to pick up the pieces and wipe off the blood, your
knees *buckle.*
Laying in the sharp mud of blood and glass you think:
Which is worse?
Failure or death?

~ 5 ~

A LITTLE WHILE

I just want to be numb. Just for a little while.
I want to muffle the outside so that everything fades away.
I *fight* and *scream* and *kick* against the urge to let everything
disappear underneath the chaos in my mind.
It is a monster, coming to snatch my feet out from underneath
me and drag me back into the darkest parts of my mind.
I throw another pill down my throat, bracing myself against the
edge of my bed as the demons whirl around me, creating a breath-
taking wind.
I know, scientifically, that this isn't a cure all.
They will come back.
But maybe before they do I can *rest*.
Maybe before they do I can *eat*.
Maybe before they do I can *breathe*.
I imagine that taking these pills are like the eye of the storm.
A moment of clean air before the world comes crashing down
around me.
A time to gather up and bear my arms.
A moment to shake off the exhaustion that clouds my eyes, a
time to tell myself that the battle only lasts for a little while.

~ 6 ~

I'M NOT TIRED

Why does no one talk about how bad it gets?
We talk about the *sadness,* the *darkness,* the *thoughts.*
We talk about not sleeping and sleeping too much.
For that, we get the simple answers like "just stop being lazy"
and "you can't choose to wallow."
What we don't talk about is the sweat pants, the unwashed hair.
Not eating because the steps to make yourself a peanut butter
and jelly sandwich is beyond the energy capacity that you hold,
and so you let your stomach churn.
What we don't talk about is forgetting to blink because your
body is so exhausted trying to keep itself alive that it glitches.
What we don't talk about is that your whole body *aches.*
What we don't talk about is knowing people can see that you're
hurting and they say *nothing.*
What we don't talk about is the abyss that comes with knowing
that no one will ever *know you, love you, hold you,*
And if they do it's because you have constructed this fake
reality of yourself and handed it to them on a silver platter, which
they gratefully gobbled up, not stopping to look and see that truly:
You are starving.
What we don't talk about is how it is not just a mental thing, is
is a monster that consumes us.

~ 7 ~

HATE MYSELF

I hate myself.
I hate the lines around my smile,
I hate the way that my eyes seem too round for my head,
I hate the way that my laugh squeaks through my teeth into the
air,
I hate the way I make others feel.
I hate the way that I feel as if I am never a victim, even if I am
holding in tears at the slicing words that spill from her mouth.
I feel like an actor when my friends tell me they love me.
When I am told I am beautiful all I can do is shake my head.
I hate myself.

~ 8 ~

BROKEN

I gave up on you a long time ago.
I whisper to myself in the mirror.
You're nothing but a piece of me, now.
A piece of something I wanted to be.
As much as I hate it, I don't know how to stop the spiral.
I look at myself and see a girl.
A girl who is scared,
a girl who is an impostor,
a girl who is nothing.

~ 9 ~

TWO PARTS

There are two parts of a human.
Who we are and who we wish to be.
There are *two parts* of a human.
The yin and yang of darkness and light.
The darkness tries to protect the light. To cover it and protect it
from the outside.
The light is smothered by the darkness and tries to banish it.
The light pushes away the darkness, and gets hit by the outside
forces.
The cycle of brokenness and fear continues.
The light, afraid of being smothered and broken,
and the dark, afraid of being banished and burned.

~ 10 ~

NO ONE CARES

"No one cares."
I tell myself for the millionth time as wipe my own mascara off
of my cheeks.
"No one cares."
I tell myself over,
and over,
and over,
So that maybe one time it'll stick and I won't want to reach out
to hands that slap mine away.
"No one cares." I whisper as my hands shake and I feel like I
can't handle the world anymore.
"You are no one's responsibility."
I tell myself when my mind starts to question why I'm so alone.
"Just handle it." I tell myself.
"Suck it up, put some big girl pants on and *handle it* because *no
one* cares and *no one's* coming to save you."

~ 11 ~

I PROMISE

I promise one day this will stop.
I'll stop crying.
I'll stop panicking.
I'll stop asking you for help because I can't help myself.
I promise one day that you won't have to worry about leaving
me at home by myself.
You won't have to pay for the medication,
the therapy,
the doctors appointments.
I'll stop apologizing for everything little thing.
I'll be better,
do better.
I'll be able to support you back.
I'll be okay.
I'll be happy.
I'll smile more,
I'll smile often.
I'll be able to control my emotions and have bad days without
wanting to hurt myself.
I promise I'll stop crying.
But I can't promise I'll stop feeling guilty.
No.

I don't think that will ever stop.

~ 12 ~

STARS IN THE NIGHT BEFORE

Even the worst days have little moments of sunshine.
At least *once a day* you do something that you take for granted.
Everyday.
Most days are bad for me.
Most days I don't see the point.
The point of life.
The point of trying.
Sometimes it's late at night, it's dark, and cold, and I can't
remember warmth. I can't remember light. I can't remember life.
So as I go through my day I acknowledge the light, I acknowl-
edge the warmth.
I breathe in the warmth of my coffee.
I remember to soak into my music, lean into it as if I am leaning
into a lover.
When my brother asks to play, his tiny fingers wrapping around
the frame of my door, I remember how I felt the night before.
Lonely. So lonely.
And I say yes.
I drudge through my day. And it's not always easy.
I write on my hands because my mind hurts me.
I write on paper because I'm scared of the dark.

As I lay down I start to spiral, but I focus on how I felt as I ran down the hills; as my feet crunched the concrete below my feet, as my ponytail whipped in the air.
These little moments bring me peace in the dark.
Even though my darkness weighs me down I still try to look up and see the stars.

~ 13 ~

I'M READY FOR THE APOCALYPSE

Stop to stop
Slow it all down
Until I can hear
Until I can breathe
Until the world strops spinning
And I can finally quiet the humming in my brain

~ 14 ~

THE SMARTEST PEOPLE

They say that the smartest people are the ones that struggle
with their mind the most.
Is it mania or does it mean that war is over?
The thought that the ones who are able to see the world most
clearly are the ones that wish to cut themselves off from it is
strange to me.
Is it depression or is it just reality?
But it makes so much sense.

~ 15 ~

DECEMBER

It's a December kind of dark.
The kind of dark that makes you exhausted.
The kind of dark that lets the monsters roam.
We don't realize how dark the world around us is until we start
to write things down.
Once we start to pour over the pages that outline the inside of
our hearts we realize that this *really is* just a desolate place where
we have all been sent to suffer.
It's always a December kind of dark,
because this is our living hell.

TRUST

They tell me that I can trust them,
Of course my first response is no,
I have learned the hard way that even the kindest people are
liars when it comes to me.
No one stays unless forced to by societal obligations.
I am convinced that if my mother saw me on the street she
would wrinkle her nose in disgust,
My father scoffs at my friends when they are a reflection of my
inner soul,
My brother rolls his eyes when he listens to my mind spin.
They love me I know that was never in the question.
I have learned the hard way that being loved and being liked
are two different things,
They tell me that I can trust them,
I nod my head and move on with my day but I know
Oh gods above do I know how terrible it is to be lied to.

~ 17 ~

RAZOR WIRE

I string razor wire through my rib-cage so that other people
can't do it first.
If I pierce my own heart,
it doesn't hurt as bad when others sink the knife deeper.
Hurting yourself makes it hurt less when others inflict harm.

~ 18 ~

BEING OPEN

My voice is not sweet like honey
My lips do not taste like plums
My skin is not soft like the butterflies wing
My laugh will grate against your ears like sandpaper
I know why people do not read my words
I am not someone who is made for the light
But as I sit in the darkness I can't help but imagine
being a person that someone wishes to listen to

~ 19 ~

MY MIND IS A WEAPON

I will not validate because I was not validated.
I will not cradle because I have never felt soft touch.
I was taught to fight like a snake,
Strike your enemy before your enemy strikes you.
Why would I lay in your lap like a cat?
I am not mother Mary, kind and soft,
I am a daughter of Athena
Raised in knowledge and war.
I may be broken but I am stronger than you ever will be.
I may be a villain but at least I'm not *weak.*

~ 20 ~

BURDEN

They told me I wasn't enough as I sat there,
Flesh rotting away from the corpse that my mother calls a
body.
Look inside my soul and see that I am unafraid
That is a lie
You see, I am terrified of my own self.
I am a burden
Taking and taking and *taking*
Until the people around me are just broken husks I used to call:
Friends.
Family.
Lovers.
They say that they love me until the time clicks out and their
eyes open and they see me in all my *broken glory*.
I am a burden
A broken person who stumbles every time she walks.
Every time I try I fail, falling back into the same beaten path
that I have walked around a thousand times,
Circles
I cry enough tears to fill the ocean while the people around me
scream loud enough to battle the winds.
I will never be the person who I manifest in the mirror.

I am a burden
and always will be.

~ 21 ~

NOTHING

Nothing
My shoulder knocks against someone's boundary, as if I had hit
a wall,
And an ache follows through it.
Next, it's my forehead against someone's annoyance,
I ping pong off people as if I am nothing,
Tethered to life as if I am a puppet on a string
I mean *nothing*
With strings around my hands and feet
No matter how hard I try I will never clear the mountain that is
the universe,
I will never get better
I will never be more than I am *right now*
Bam
My body crumples against the weight of somebody's dis-
appointment in me
I am nothing
I think,
As I lay here, broken and bloody, my cheek against the un-
forgiving dirt, spitting broken words to seal my broken heart, my
tongue flicking against the ashes
Nothing

$$\sim 22 \sim$$

THE RAMBLINGS OF A BROKEN WOMAN

My *mind never rests* a constant and dreadful spinning,
We are *nothing* but dust and shadows.
I fling out my arms and embrace death with sharp thorns
cradling my shoulders like a forgotten lover.
The universe has forsaken me like all of the other gods before
me,
You must *give* to get and I have been *selfish*
My pain is self inflicted but it hurts all the same.
I have this *dream* that one day I will meet another broken
person,
And our jagged pieces will line up and create something whole
Someone beautiful
Like a stained glass window, different colors shining in all
different directions,
But that is mad.
Because only death can answer my call for help

~ 23 ~

THE MOTHER'S

The mother's are sick.
My mother's genes are a cancer inside of my body.
Crazy how the one that brought you into this life is the one that makes you want to leave it the most.
I go to bed thinking of cracking necks and broken spines.
I wake up my eyes fluttering open to the sound of still lungs.
It will never end.
My mother runs a finger across the arch of my eyebrow and my eyelashes touch my cheek as she tells me to stop picking at my face, it will scar.
This eternal torment,
it is in my genes, my DNA.
She was broken, a doll used for their amusement so she must break me too.
It is only fair.
I cannot run from it.
The sickness is in our bones,
And when I become a mother,
I will do the same thing to my daughter,
And the daughter she bares,
The mothers are broken.

~ 24 ~

IS THIS HOW LUCIFER FELT?

Is Lucifer my name?
You expect me to be good,
To be pretty,
To be *perfect*.
You expect me to care to want *peace* to want *quiet*.
I am not.
I am sick of pretending and forcing myself into your unreach-
able standards.
I recognize that I am creating chaos but sometimes being
noticed in the chaos is better than nothing at all.
You created me this way, making me hate my own self until I
hated everything around me.
You make me feel as if I would be better rotting underneath the
ground and then snarl your nose when I cannot love you as you
wish for me to.
I pant, fiery air filling my lungs as I huff with anger,
And all I can think of as you sit here and scream your dis-
appointment is:
Lucifer is my name.

~ 25 ~

THE WORLD

It's crazy how the world works.
It gives you a suicidal daughter and a son who breaks his own
bones at the mention of grief.
I carry my family name like football pads: heavy and ashamed,
but acting like it is something I can be proud of, in reality it is
simply another dangerous thing I thrust myself into and act like it
is fun.

I go into an interview and the manager calls my mother to tell
her I got the job.
No one tells her how I sit in the dark terrified of reaching out
because I burn everything I touch.
It's crazy how the world works.
It is broken in the most complex ways.
Mothers make you suicidal and fathers make you homicidal.

And then you see someone who has grown up *without hurt*, her
name is Rachel and she is the epitome of perfect:
blonde hair and a button nose and a father who comes into her
work and compliments her on her smile.

She says she will pray for me, which means that she has not
gone through the painstaking failure of deconstructing the re-
ligion she was built upon.
And you can't help but think that maybe it's me, *us, we* that are
broken this family of misfits and broken spare toys.
But that is just the shattered mirror pieces of the world reflect-
ing back on you.
It's crazy how the world works.

~ 26 ~

KNIFE POINT OF DEATH

The ghost told us to fuck off.
We laid our heads on it's grave.
He succumbed to my own demons;
I was a ghost, walking through the halls as if in preparation for
what I would have seen if I had laid down all those years ago.
It hurts.
Knowing that I saw,
Knowing that I was,
Knowing we never discussed.
Guilt eats away at my bones the way that a fly eats away at the
rot from a fruit.
My fear kept me from reaching out. From laying my demons
down.
Maybe since my demons were the same, our demons would
have battled each other instead of throwing us toward the razor
sharp knife point between life and death.
We laid our heads on his grave,
He told us to fuck off.

~ 27 ~

BONES

Once again it is in our bones.
A thrumming in my head, *go*
I thought I had the ability to get out
A broken mysterious illness we cannot see but feel everyday
Go
I want to escape the strands of my DNA, rip them off like chains
off a prisoner
Go
Those who dance are thought to be insane by those who do not
hear the music
Go
"Salu bitch!" My mom yells, raising a glass in a toast to the
strong bond of generational curses tying us to the ground
Go
I can't get out. I can't breathe I can't leave it behind. It will
follow me six feet under the ground and into another dimension
Go
I can feel it in my bones.

~ 28 ~

MY EULOGY

I play this game with myself.
What will they say, when they lay me in the ground?
Would they speak of my love for coffee?
Would they tell everyone about the stories that I created?
Would they speak of my pain?
I play this game with myself, and I lose every time.
Surely, they would not speak of how I used my tongue as a
knife,
Surely, they would not speak of how I closed my self harder
than a windblown door.
I play this game with myself, and I lose every time.

~ 29 ~

LAVENDER TEA

The monster crawls back up my throat, stealing my breath.
I fight it off with a cup of lavender tea, a hot bath.
But it laughs.
"Practice self care." They say.
"Depression is a state of mind that can be willed into submission."
My achy muscles *wince* at the thought of opening my eyes in the morning.
Someone looks me in the eyes for too long and they start to water.
"Broken" the monster whispers, as I force myself to take a walk.
I keep a notebook labeled 'reasons to stay' under my pillow.
The first line on it is "so that my mother..." *I'll let you fill in the blanks.*
Angel of death takes life with kisses.
I know what a sweet relief leaving will bring *me* but what about *everyone else?*
So when the monster crawls up my throat, past the sockets of my eyeballs, pressure breaking my brain with the force of my emotions.
I fight it off with a hot bath, and lavender tea.

AUTHOR'S NOTE

My family can track neuro-divergent genes back four generations. We have had three generations contain a person who took their own life, because of their mental struggles.

There is a lot of pain that travels when such a thing happens, especially when it is a genetic struggle. It is a unique feeling, wondering if one day you might be next. It is even worse to wonder, if not you, who else?

I want to note that there are some poems in this collection with no punctuation, because I wanted to convey the feeling of being rushed, or having a long winded experience. That is what my life has been, a long winded experience. When I talk to others that also struggle with topics such as depression or anxiety, they have conveyed feeling like they are weightless, being pushed forward in time against their own will. "Suicide isn't an option". That has always been a mantra of mine. I don't get to make that decision, regardless of how painful it is.

Although, in my ultimate world, I would disappear and no one would be harmed. I'm sure everyone reading this collection can agree with that feeling.

I wrote this collection partly for myself, partly for my family, but also partly for those who haven't had the history of family to tether them to the ground.

There are others out there, just like you, and we need you here.

I also want to make a note that while, *yes* I have had difficulties in the past, I wrote this with a character in mind. I wrote this from the point of view if I were to have an unreliable narrator at hand. Which, for some, we *are* unreliable narrators when it comes to mental illness. We can't always trust ourselves, or our thoughts, and I wanted to show that in this book.

Thank you for reading this book, and remember, you are not alone.